SILVER LINING

AYUSHI NARAYAN

Made with ♥ on the Notion Press Platform
www.notionpress.com

To me for I found solace in these poems.

Contents

Contents

I can barely conceive of a type of beauty in which there is no melancholy.

- Charles Baudelaire

Preface

The book 'Silver Lining' consists of fifty poems that came straight from my heart. The poems in this book are simply my emotions that I have endeavored to capture in their purest form on paper. The poems discuss various aspects of life such as nature, various colors, our feelings, our parents, and so on. I attempted to creatively discuss these basic topics.

The majority of the poems are composed in free verse, without a particular rhyme pattern, in order to establish a conversational atmosphere that makes it simple for everyone to comprehend the messages I aim to convey in the poem. Most of the poems in this book conclude with an optimistic and joyful ending. I penned many of these poems during a dark period in my life when I was feeling low, but being the eternal optimist that I am, I searched for a glimmer of hope.

I hope that by the conclusion of reading this book, you will feel empowered, content, increasingly positive, and eager to embrace life, just as I did after writing these poems.

Acknowledgements

I would like to express my gratitude to life and the many hurdles and tests it made me attempt, and I would also like to thank my patience and my perseverance because without either I wouldn't have been inspired to write neither would I have had it in me to write a book.

I would also like to thank all my English teachers till date whom I vividly remember because all of them have played a significant role in developing my writing style even though some of them just scolded me for making silly grammatical errors, I have learnt a lot from them and still hope wish to continue to learn a lot more.

Last but not the least, I would like to thank my parents and everything around me(flowers, ceramic bowls) because they really inspired me.

I would also like to thank the Sun and the Moon because whenever I look at them I feel at peace and feel motivated to write more(they probably will never read this but I need to thank them).

1. The Fairy And The Secret To Success

Once upon a time,
There lived a child,
Who wanted to be great,
But she only slept and ate.
She believed that one day she would achieve greatness,
That one day she would achieve great things,
Even though all she did was eat, sleep and dream.
One day, a little fairy flew up to her face,
She flew past her eyes,
And past her hair,
To her ear and the child heard a little voice
That said-
"Oh little child!
Oh little child!
All you do is eat, sleep and dream all day and night,
Do you still believe that you will achieve great things in your life?"
The little child replied in the affirmative,
And the fairy continued with her speech,
"My little child,
Those who are great,
Stay awake,
And strive.
They don't only dream about the great things they wish to achieve in life.

They work instead of dreaming,
They struggle and strive to win instead of dreaming,
They study instead of dreaming,
You see my little girl,
They work,
Because they know that if they do so,
What they dream of will be their future."
The little fairy then flew away, her wings shining,
And she left the little child pondering.
The next day the little girl was no longer seen dreaming,
She had started studying!
So, my dear readers,
To achieve what you wish to,
You need to get out of bed,
You need to stop procrastinating,
And start working.
And trust me if you do so,
You will achieve all that you wish for.

2. Teenagehood

I am two years into teenage hood,
And I have been enjoying it.
I have gotten used to the mood shifts,
And the fluctuating levels of dopamine.
I have come to make peace with the occasional, "Life sucks",
And the most frequent "I don't care at all".
I have realized that life isn't a fairy tale,
It's more of a rocky pathway where it usually rains.
I have accepted that life won't always go the way I want it to,
My plans can fail and they usually do.
But I have found sunlight even in this dark room,
I have found several reasons to smile during the monsoon.
I have learnt to take life as it comes,
In its raw and unaltered forms.
I have learnt to not make changes,
And have realized that everything can't be perfect.
I have found beauty in my flaws,
Like my acne; it's not bad at all.
I have realized that first comes sadness and then joy follows,
It's a rule that stays the same for all.
I have learnt to trust even after being betrayed,
Believing that everyone is built different.
I have learnt to rectify my mistakes,
Instead of repeating them again and again.
These two years sometimes felt like two decades and sometimes like

two days,
Time flew fast and sometimes it felt like it didn't move at all.
I felt love and hatred.
And most importantly I learnt to take life as it comes,
And to not overthink it all.

3. New Day, New Me

Some days you can be a mess,
Some days you can be perfect.
Some days you can be angry,
While the others you can be happy.
Some days you can be depressed,
Whilst the others you can be a total crackhead.
Because there are three hundred and sixty-five days in a year,
It would be boring to be the same each day,
So be different every day.
Be special,
Be common,
Stand out and blend in.
Be unique,
Be like the rest,
Just be yourself.
Somedays,
You can laugh continuously,
Or you can shed tears for hours.
You can yell at people and be angry
Or you can just stay calm.
The goal is to be different each day,
Be a better or a worse version of yourself every other day.
Be different every day.
Change your expressions as if they are a piece of clothing,
Once you start doing that, trust me your life will never be boring.

4. Incompatible Pieces

Some people are just not meant for each other,
They are like pieces of a puzzle,
That belong to two different corners.
No matter how hard you try to make them fit,
They never will.
Instead you will only end up breaking a part of each,
Because some things are just not meant to be.
And even if you succeed in putting them together,
You will certainly notice the little cracks in between,
Because they were never meant to meet.

5. Mother Nature

I am not an orphan,
All of nature is my mother.
When it thunders my mother scolds me for making stupid decisions,
When it rains, it's my mother giving me a cold, refreshing bath.
The cool breeze running through my hair and calming my entire body
are her hands pulling me into an embrace.
The shining sun is her bright smile,
That could light up and fill every part of me.
The lakes are her eyes,
Emerald green and so deep,
Just looking at them rids me of all my worries.
The night sky is her glowing skin,
So calm with stars twinkling.
The plants that lie on her lap,
They are all my siblings.
Who says I am an orphan,
I have a mother,
A mighty and strong one,
She is mother nature.

6. Unanswered Question

I wonder what it feels like to jump off the top of a building knowing that when you reach it's foot you are going to die,
I wonder what it feels like to delibrately try taking your own life,
I wonder what it feels like to walk into the light.
I wonder what it takes for one to leave their loved ones behind and just die,
I wonder what the magnitude of pain a person must be subjected to, to propel one to give up on life.
I wonder,
And so I ponder.
Trying to find out the reason,
An answer.
Is it because you are tired of trying?
Or because you are tired of disappointing everyone?
Or maybe its because you are just tired of living?
Perhaps its because you are exhausted of pretending to smile when deep inside you are weeping.
But I never find an answer that justifies this action,
And this remains an unanswered question.

7. Live

I am happy to be alive,
I am happy to be breathing after all I have been through in life
I am glad I held on to the little hope I had,
I am glad I didn't let it fly away in the wind like the red balloon I loved did.
There were times when I couldn't see the light,
When I thought it'd be better to die.
But now I see it clearly,
The light shining happily.
I thought it'd rain forever,
However I am glad I waited for the summer.
Because now I can run through the field of sunflowers.
And I can sit at the beach waiting for the water to touch my feet.
I am glad I lived to see the sun rise the next day,
Because if I hadn't I would have never known what was waiting for me ahead.
I would have thought I was doomed,
But I am glad I lived because I am blessed.
I am glad I waited for the summer instead of ending my story in the rain,
Because I met you, my friend.
I met my reason to live,
And so I will.
Now, I shall live for many years,
Until my body grows so fragile that it perishes,

And my life ends.
So live,
Live to see the summer or the winter,
Live to see your favourite season,
Live to see your favourite flower bloom,
Live to feel the wind fight and try to push you.
Live to see the stars at night,
And live to see the sunrise.
Try living for these little things,
And before you realise you will love living.

8. Love

They say Sanskrit is the oldest language in the world,
But I believe it is love.
For what other way would you tell a person you'd keep them safe,
Than pull them into a warm embrace and plant a kiss on their face.
It's true that love is the oldest language,
It existed in the Garden of Eden.
Adam and Eve knew it,
They didn't need to speak or use words,
Because they knew something a lot more magical-- love.
Words don't win a person's heart,
It's the emotions and affection with which they are spoken.
And so it's proven again,
That love is not just the oldest language but in fact the most impactful one.

9. Paradoxical Love

When you love someone,
You hate them,
But you are also the first one to show up when they are in pain and help them.
When you love someone,
You feel like killing them,
But you are also ready to take the fall for them if needed.
When you love someone,
You despise them,
But you also miss them badly when you don't get to see them.
When you love someone,
You are ready to hurt them,
But it's always for their welfare.

10. Bare Minimum

They say don't settle for the bare minimum,
But what if the bare minimum is all I've ever known.
What if my parents and family members,
Always provided me with the bare minimum.
Then won't a guy smiling at me be enough to make my heart flutter?
Won't it be enough to make me fall in love and plan our future?
And they call me delusional.
But to me the bare minimum is the maximum.

11. My Prince

How am I supposed to believe?
That in a world where divorce exists,
I will find love like they do in the movies and the stories.

How do I believe?
That I will be saved by a prince,
Who will come to me on a white horse and take me with him.

How do I believe?
That I will have my happily ever after,
Especially when tears follow laughter.

Maybe I should stop being a damsel in distress,
And find my own way out of this mess.
I will be the prince to my soul,
And protect myself from the dangers all alone.

Because my prince may leave me,
Once he sees the real me,
So it'd be way better if I am my own prince.

12. Loved-Unloved

I learnt to love you,
Even the bad you,
Then I learnt to unlove you,
Even the good you.

My mentor was time,
It taught me how to forget your eyes,
Your lies,
And your lips,

Now I barely remember your face,
Just pieces of a puzzle scattered here and there,
Whenever I try to picture your face, putting the fragments piece by piece,
I always end up with nothing.

13. My Sun

I remember how you taught me English,
I remember how we used to sit in the garden when I was sick.
I remember you planting your favourite flowers,
And I remember you watering them during the evening hours.
You were like the sunlight,
Always shining through the dark.
You were a flower that never wilted,
And to me you were like a sun that'd never set.
But it hurts,
To see what you've become.
You only went away for a week,
But it seems like you were tortured for an eternity.
Life has never been easy on you mother,
But you were always stronger than any problem.
You'd smile through the pain,
And you'd laugh the tears away.
Whenever I felt scared you'd hide me from the world in your warm embrace.
But what happened to you now,
You are no longer shining through the dark,
It feels like you have given up.
You no longer smile through the pain,
Instead you let the tears win.
I know it was hard,
But if only you held for a little longer,

You'd be here to see that it worked.
That life didn't disappoint us.
It gave us what we deserved.
But you aren't here mother,
You aren't here to see the sunrise,
You aren't here to see the waves crashing,
You aren't here to feel the breeze hugging every part of your body.
You didn't make it through the hike,
I wish you would have seen the sunrise from this height.

14. Eternal Promise

I look up at the sky,
I look at the stars in the night sky,
And I wonder,
Which of these is you, my mother?
I look at them with all my affection,
And I look at them with all my love for you,
The affection I would have drowned you with,
If only you were still here.
I have looked for you everywhere,
Somehow I can't believe the fact that you're gone,
Forever.
People tell me that I am in denial,
But that's not true,
Because you had promised me that you would always be by my side,
Till the day I die.
And you are a woman of your word,
You haven't broken a promise, never.
So, I am still looking for you.
I asked the sea, the wind, the sun,
Now I look for your bright, glowing eyes among the many twinkling stars,
Hoping I see them again.
I miss you mother,
I miss your hugs,
And I miss your wise words.

I will keep looking for you,
Because I know you keep your promises when you say so,
You do.

15. Dandelion

You are like a dandelion,
You open up when it's bright,
And you close in the evening when there's no light.
Why can't you stay strong,
Why do you only think that things will go wrong.
You hide yourself when life starts getting tough,
Why don't you realise that *you* can be tougher.
I wonder, why you are so fragile,
Pretty things can be strong too,
They can be brave and courageous,
So why do you hide,
When there's no light.
Get out of your hellhole,
Look at the world outside,
It is cruel and evil, I know,
But you can't be afraid of it,
You are more than what you see,
You aren't a coward,
You are brave,
Just give yourself a chance,
And you will see that you can fight,
You can make it through life,
Even when there's no light.

16. Invisible Wounds

Whenever I told people about the real me,
They'd say goodbye and end everything.
They'd end everything they had with me,
Because they saw how broken I was inside,
They realised that I was a hypocrite,
And who I was in front of them was all a lie.
So they'd end things with me,
As if they were merely
Pulling out a loose cloth fibre from their favourite dress, and not very gently.
They left the surroundings of the fabric stretched.
They'd end all that we ever had,
They'd tear our relationship as if it were paper.
They'd end things with me,
As if I was never human.
They always left before I cried,
They never saw my tears rolling down my cheek at night.
When I asked them, why they all ended things with me,
They'd say because my pretty smile was a lie,
Because *I* wasn't human inside.
They'd say it all in one breath,
Not realising that it was them,
Who made me who I am today,
They made me a monster, a devil, a cold-blooded human, a corpse somehow breathing.

All they saw was what I have become,
All they asked was what I was.
They never asked me how I became that thing,
They never asked me who forced me to become it.
All they did was ending things with me.

17. The A1 Love

Someone asked me-
Why do I study?
I said that it was a good question,
and set out on a journey,
To discover my reasons for studying.

I ruled out all the possibilities-
Do I study to be successful?
Or maybe my reason to study,
Is to earn lots of money.
Perhaps my reason for studying
Is to become someone I dream of becoming.

But then it struck me,
The force that made me study,
The right reason.
I study to get my dad's approval,
To receive his love,
To see him smile,
When the teachers tell him that I am a perfect child.

However, after all these years of studying,
I still haven't received a heartfelt hug from him.

18. Love Hurts

Love hurts,
I know none of you will believe me, but trust me it does.
It hurts to love someone.
All types of love,
They hurt.
Whether it be unrequited love or the mutual one,
Both of them hurt,
But you never feel the pain,
For love is a sweet poison,
It's as sweet as honey,
But it's a poison after all,
It's not harmless.
Mutual love hurts too,
When you love someone,
You suppress your own desires to fulfill theirs,
In this way, you forget your true self,
You change yourself,
Though you never meant to.
You love your lover more than you love yourself,
You depend on them,
You wait for them to love you,
But self-love is important too.
However you forget,
And if this isn't harming yourself,
Then what is?

The sweet moments make you forget the bitter, painful experiences,
But that doesn't mean that they never existed,
They were just hidden.
Just lost,
But never gone.
Unrequited love,
It sucks.
I'd say that it hurts the most.
It makes you feel as if your head is being banged against a rocky mountain,
But you cherish the pain.
When you love someone,
And realise that they might not feel the same,
You get up in the morning everyday,
And look into the mirror at your reflection and say," I must lack something, it must be me, the problem is me".
You starve yourself to death,
You run until you are out of breath,
All in order to make yourself look different,
To make someone love someone, who isn't you.
You change yourself for someone who has never noticed you,
All for what?
For the sweet poison that you wish to taste,
To drink the poison from your lover's hand with every kiss you guys share?
You harm yourself every day,
For someone who will never care.
I don't know about others,
But from my experiences, I'd say love hurts,

All types of love,
They all hurt.

19. Until Life Do Us Part

Most people say," Until death do us part".
But I will say," Until life do us part",
Because it's the things in life that will drive a wedge between us,
It's those fights about the chores or splitting of taxes that will ruin our love,
It isn't death,
Because the thought of you dying makes me want you back,
But the thought of living with you makes me run in the opposite direction.
Death is all but a mere escape,
For some it's a new beginning.
It's life that will test our love and eventually we will fail,
Because no matter what one does,
Situations in life end up drastically changing us, teaching us things,
And in the end we lose ourselves and our so-called eternal love.
Death just keeps that love eternal,
Because after one's death,
We pine for them,
And our love for them only grows.

20. Unlike Me

I don't want him to feel the same pain,
The pain I felt when I was his age.
I don't want his happiness to be snatched from him,
His right to a happy life.
I don't want his Christmas gift list to be torn into pieces,
I don't want his dreams to die,
I want them to shine bright.
I don't want his happy time to be interrupted.
I don't want him to be traumatized,
I want him to live a carefree life.
I don't want him to feel imprisoned,
I want him to feel free in this world.
I want him to live life,
I want him to feel safe,
I want him to feel happy and great,
I want him to live carefreely,
Not carefully like I did.
I want him to love life and truly live it,
I don't want him to be dying every second he lives,
Like I did.

21. The Unbreakable Color

I wonder why people say that black isn't a good colour,
When it endures everything,
When it is capable of dissolving all colours in it,
When it has been through all sorts of pain,
And yet has remained itself.
It is resilient!
Black is a strong colour!
However, society has always hated such things.
Things that were strong and didn't give in to obstacles easily.
It prefers things that are easy to mould and change,
Things like clay,
Like ceramic plates.
You touch it aggressively and it breaks,
Shatters into pieces.
The society prefers colours like white,
Because it is fragile,
All you require is one drop of any colour to corrupt or influence it,
To change it,
To ruin or break it.
This is what the society likes.

22. Growing

I have grown up,
But only physically.
My mind is still stuck in,
And longs to relive my childhood memories.
I have been getting less sleep,
And lots of stress.
I have been feeling less happy,
And crying almost everyday.
I feel confused and scared,
I constantly feel nervous and stared at.
I feel insecure but sometimes brave.
I feel purposeless.
I feel like dying,
But I also feel like living every second.
I tell myself that life will unfold itself,
But I keep growing impatient.
I feel scared of failing,
Even though I tell myself there's going to be tons of opportunities,
I feel desperate to win,
But I keep losing.
I think I shouldn't overthink,
And let life do its magic.

23. Not Just A Mother

I thought I hated her,
But in fact I loved her,
Perhaps a little too much.
I loved her from the bottom of my heart,
So much that whenever we bickered,
It always broke my heart,
It made me feel the pain that one feels when they are ripped apart.
I wish I had the courage,
To tell her that she's my life.
I wish my ego would take a vacation,
Whenever we argued,
So I could tell her that I am sorry,
And kiss her and bid her goodnight.
I wish I could tell her,
I wish I was brave enough to tell her,
That she's the love of my life,
That she's my one and only.
She's not just my mother,
She's my friend,
My sister,
My lover,
My partner in crime,
She's *My life,*
She's my everything.
She's not just my mother,

She's my life line,
If something happens to her,
I will certainly die.

24. Tears

I locked my tears in a locker,
And now that I want to shed them,
I have forgotten the password.
I have tried to break the locker with a hammer,
I have tried my best to get them back.
But I have been unsuccessful,
And now I regret hiding them.
I regret hiding them because now I feel like shedding them,
But there's nothing to shed.
I feel like crying my heart out,
But then I realised that I bottled them up,
And I can't open the bottle now.
It is as if the ridges and grooves of the bottle are stuck to the cap,
And so all my efforts to open it make no difference.
I feel something hard in my heart,
I feel something stuck in my throat,
And all of this will disappear,
Once I shed a few tears.

25. Cry

I cried today,

I *cried today* for the first time after weeks of assuring myself that I am strong and I won't cry at all because you are gone.

But I couldn't control the tears,

They didn't ask for my permission,

Instead they just barged their way out of the windows to my soul.

They freed themselves from the prison where I had held them hostage,

And they let out a victorious roar while doing so,

Making me weep and sob and miss you.

26. Imposter

It was a cloudy night,
The moon was shining very bright,
Looking innocent and milky white.
When I looked at it,
It reminded me of that night,
When my dad narrated the story of the little witch,
The pretty witch,
Who was fourteen.
She was evil and cruel,
And she hid among the human beings.
Her blue eyes always gleamed in innocence,
But it was something she had never known.
She was the epitome of an imposter,
A wolf hiding amongst the sheep,
In a costume she did steal.
The moon too stole the sun's rays,
Made it his,
And now it provides bright rays,
So,we say that it's the moon shining bright,
But the moon just owns something that never belonged to him,
Stealing someone else's credits.

27. Father

I tried my best to understand him,
To understand what goes on in his mind,
But he was the most twisted person I'd ever met,
Until today.
I finally understood him,
And realized that he is just like me.
He doesn't let his emotions show,
He hides them all the time.
Whenever he feels happy or achieves something he feels like jumping or flying,
But he keeps that hidden.
He doesn't let the tears roll down his cheeks even if he feels like crying,
He never smiles wholeheartedly,
Because deep down he is afraid,
That one day he will just be abandoned.
He lost his parents at a young age,
And since then he had to act tough,
To survive in this scary world,
And that's when he learnt to hide everything,
Until it broke him.

28. Night Sky

I don't know why,
But I find solace in the night sky,
I feel at peace when I see the stars twinkling,
And my heart flutters whenever I see the moon shining.
So, when everybody's asleep at night,
I sneak out into the balcony just to adore the sky.
I let the cool breeze free me of all my worries,
And I let the moon see me grinning.
I let the trees talk to me,
And I let the stars stare at me,
Because I know that they don't judge me,
They just adore someone who adores them.

29. Write

I write at night,
When everyone's fast asleep,
And there's not a soul roaming out on the streets.
I write to untangle the tangled yarn of thoughts in my head.
I write to calm the violent storm in my heart.
I write to relieve the stress,
And I write to feel less scared.
I write to share my thoughts,
That I know I will never be able to talk about.
I write to feel content,
And I write to impress people.
I,
I write to *live*,
To smile,
To cry.
I write so that I don't bottle up my emotions and die.
I write to survive.

30. Regret

Regret, if you have felt it you know it hurts,
Because it reminds you of all the things you did,
That you shouldn't have done.
It doesn't let you shed tears,
Because you had the chance but you messed it all up,
You threw that opportunity away,
You closed that open door,
You were the one who turned around that door knob,
But now you just wish you had a chance to change it,
You wish that you had taken the opportunity,
You wish that you had never closed that door,
Because after all you knew where it would take you,
But due to fears or reasons unknown,
You refused to take that path,
And now you regret it all.

31. Let go

Today, that obstruction rose agin in my throat,
I tried my best to suppress it,
So I gulped,
And now I am left wondering what I will do tomorrow?
Will I keep suppressing it?
Will I keep swallowing and hiding it?
Perhaps I will.
I will because I can't face it.
Because I can't surrender myself to the pain,
I can't let vestiges of me float away,
I need to hold onto the stronger me,
I need to do so to keep living.
No matter how much I want to let go,
I just can't bring myself to do so,
Perhaps it's because,
I believe something good awaits me,
But you never know life might just be waiting to hurt me.
It might want to hurt me a lot more,
So much that I finally let go.

32. Disappointment

Everyone was disappointed in me,
All because I couldn't score forty on forty.
I was just two marks behind,
And everyone started hating me since that night.
Everyone I ever knew- my parents, my teachers and my friends,
Started looking down on me and asked me what had happened.
And this is what I wanted to say to everyone's faces:
"I am a human!
And for your kind information,
Humans make errors,
But they also fix them later.
I am not supernatural,
I am just like you all.
So please spare me the pressure,
And let me live my life with a little pleasure."

33. Home

I am back home,
I am back from the roads unknown to the ones that I know,
I have come back to the sapling I planted before going away from home.
It's funny how time passes by,
The sapling I planted is now a tree almost touching the sky,
My once newly painted house is now weary and fragile.
My brother once used to run around the lawn,
Now he sits, staring at his phone.
My parents whose voices echoed in the halls,
They don't even speak anymore.
I regret leaving home,
I regret going to places unknown,
I wish I would just have stayed at home,
Because then I wouldn't have missed my brother's first day at school,
Or the day he graduated.
If I never left,
I would have been by my parent's side,
When they died,
I would have lent a shoulder to my brother to cry on.
I regret it all,
I regret leaving home.

34. True Love

When people ask me if I have experienced true love,
I say no,
Because if what we had was true love,
It would have worked out, right?
We would still be seeing each other,
You would still be cuddling me to sleep,
You would still want to hug me.
If what we had was true love,
You would still bring me ice cream at three in the morning,
You would still be helping me fall asleep.
You would still cook breakfast for me.
And I would adore you smiling,
As you served me the food you cooked,
And you would still give me a hug before going to work.
You would still love the stretch marks on my body,
You would still love me yapping,
And always talking.
If what we had was true love,
You would never tell me to shut up,
And you would always chuckle,
Whenever I thought out loud,
Or giggled.
If what we had was true love,
We would have worked it all out.

35. Phoenix

I watched you die.
I watched you as you cried.
I watched as the fire gobbled you up,
I just stood there watching as you were breathing your last breath,
I watched you screaming in pain,
I watched your skin melt,
I watched you trying to reach out for help,
However I did nothing and just stood there.
I am sorry,
That I could do nothing to stop the fire, the problem,
I apologise for not running to you when you needed me and for just standing there and watching you scream.
I saw a tear roll down your cheek,
I am sorry for not being there to wipe it.
I am sorry for not holding your hand,
When you needed me to hold it.
I apologise for running away,
And I know that you hate it.
But please forgive me,
Because I was immature.
I was a kid so I didn't know how to deal with it.
Please forgive me,
For running away from the problems,
And leaving you alone to face them,
I should have been by your side,

But you see I was afraid to face life.
I know you won't forgive me,
But I hope that now you are somewhere, smiling.
Because now you know now that I didn't abandon you,
I was just scared that I might hurt you,,
So I ran away from you,
And left you alone.
Like the brave person you were,
You emerged stronger,
From the fire,
Just like a phoneix does.
Just know that I is proud of you my brother.

36. Empty

I have been feeling empty,
Like there's something missing in me,
And I don't know how to fill it,
I don't know how to fill the hollow space in me.
Every night I look at your pictures,
Hoping that doing so will relieve me,
But it doesn't work,
The hunger to meet you only burns more than it did once.
I look in the mirror,
To see the eyes you gave me, mother.
Hoping that doing so would decrease the pain I have been feeling ever since your departure,
But all I see are those eyes brimming up with tears.
There's nothing in me,
Nothing at all,
I had a soul,
But now it seems to have gone.
They say the soul stays where the loved one lives,
So it looks like it's with you, mum.
And since you aren't here,
I have been feeling empty as my soul's wherever you are.

37. Like Poles of The Magnet

I don't like my family.
Honestly, I am not lying,
And things between us will never be fine.

Call me a pessimist,
But the truth shall remain still,
Nothing between us will ever change.
Like it or not, it is what it is.

We fight every night,
And then we all hide and cry.
Next morning we smile,
Pretending not to remember what happened last night.

We all wish for each other to die,
We tell them to die while smiling,
We are like magnets that face the like pole,
We repel,
And anything you do will never change the results

38. Dark and Twisted

I can't be a shiny, happy person,
Because I am all twisted and dark,
There's a shadow lurking in my heart.
I try my best to smile and put on a show,
To make sure I am liked by all.
But I am different with the people I love,
At the places that are familliar.
I talk about death like its better than life,
I have tried dying,
I cry before sleeping,
I don't pretend to smile with those who truly know me.
I don't put on a facade,
I remain my dark and twisted self.

39. Silver Lining

Every cloud has a silver lining.
There are nights when you can't sleep,
But there'll be nights when you will sleep peacefully.
There are days when you can't eat,
But there'll be days when you will have and throw a feast.
Because every cloud has a silver lining,
After every thunderstorm the sun rises.
Each sunset has always been followed by a sunrise.
Each teardrop leads to a laughter in the future.
Even the darkest, moisture-laden cloud has a silver lining,
To see it all you need to do is give it some time.

40. Death

Death isn't scary,
It's just the end of a beautiful journey.
Death is just the end of a person's experiences.
It's the end of being broken but collecting the pieces and rebuilding yourself,
It's the end of loving someone more than you could have ever loved yourself,
It's the end of being hated and being loved,
It's the end of falling down and getting up,
It's the end of reliving the same life and often doing something different.
Death is leaving your loved ones behind but going to the ones that left you once upon a time.
Death is the end of everything you have experienced- the good, the bad, the things you hated and the ones you loved.
Death is the end of your beautiful experiences here on earth.
Death is the inevitable end that one must accept.

41. Death- An easy way out

I think death is an escape from hardships,
It's an easy way out,
Or at least it seems like it is.
Death is the back door,
You take it to sneak out at night when things are bad,
You hide and run away.
Death is a shortcut,
It's that route where you skip the obstacles, the future and get something that feels like peace.
Death is tempting,
It is easier to die than to live,
But death is also missing out on everything good and bad, happy and sad.
Death is skipping the obstacles along with the to come happy memories.
Death is a cheat sheet,
It might give you peace but it isn't the right path.
Death is easy and life is hard,
But after living through the hardships,
You smile the brightest.

42. Scars

We all have scars,
Some are just fresh and plump,
While others have healed over the years.
Some of our scars run so deep that even after a few decades pass,
They don't heal or change at all.
We all have scars,
And we all try to hide them,
Because we have always been taught that our scars are our weaknesses,
And one must never show that, as humans they are vulnerable.
We all have scars,
And it is always our loved ones who give them to us.
And we all readily get hurt,
Because being hurt by your loved ones has been normalized,
Being your family's punching bag has been normalized,
And you have been taught to never raise your voice,
Or tell them to stop,
Even if it means that you die.

43. New You

There are times when I don't like the new you,
So I just keep replaying the memories of the old you.
And as I replay them in my head over and over again,
You think that I have zoned out and am not paying attention to you again.
But how do I tell you,
That this new you is amazing but, it isn't the version of t you that I used to know.
This isn't the version of you that I loved.
I apologise if I am rude or selfish,
But to me, this isn't the real you,
So I am sorry if I let go of you.

44. Red Thread

They say that there is an invisible red thread that connects us to the one we are destined to meet,
But what if I was just destined to be alone,
What if that red thread was just tied to my other hand,
What if I was destined to meet a better, new me.
What if my red thread isn't tied to anyone else but me,
Wouldn't it be lonely?
And what if I am an island?
Some people say that being left alone is the best feeling,
But what if you were left alone for too long,
And now you crave company,
But no one understands you, no one wants to get to know you,
What if everyone hates you,
And you just come back to yourself,
And find that the other end of the red thread was tied to the index finger of your left hand.

45. On The Brink

Almost
What a tragic word!
It means: not quite or nearly, but not completely.
I was almost happy.
I almost reached the top.
I almost succeeded.
I almost won.
I almost did something but I never actually did it.
I wish this word never existed!
Because it tells you that you were so close yet so far,
It tells you that you were just a hair's breadth away from something,
Your fingers slipping through the cracks.
You nearly achieved something but missed it- Close! But no cigar!
You almost got it,
Almost!
However, sometimes I am glad that it exists,
Because there are times like these-
'I alomst died,
I almost lost my mind.'
These are the times when I am glad this word exists,
Because it tells you about the numerous possibilities,
All you have to do is change the way you see things!

46. Diamonds

I finally understood why diamonds are more precious than other jewels:
It's because diamonds shine even when a tiny ray of light falls on it!
All you need is a weeny source of light,
And they shall shine bright.
Diamonds show people the tiny ray of hope in their darkest times.
They shine and lead the people away from the dark, sad ruins of life.
Diamonds shine bright, they give hope, they show people life.
Diamonds help people survive.
And did you know that diamonds have a high melting point,
Even when they are subjected to lots of heat,
They fight,
They survive.
Other metals and gemstones need more than just a ray of light to shine this way,
And so they can't show people the hopeful way,
So maybe that's why they are less precious than diamonds.
We are all diamonds!

47. Ceramic Bowl

I am a ceramic bowl,
I am delicate yet so beautiful,
I am fragile but I am still quite strong.
He holds me;
His hands so soft and warm.
My shiny, smooth surface in contact with his hands as soft as a pillow and as warm as a sunbeam on your skin.
(I feel safe.)
His touch feels like a gentle hug.
Suddenly, his hands turn cold as a dead man's nose,
And his hands begin to shake and tremble.
(I am scared.)
He drops me,
And I break into a hundred tiny pieces,
Each piece of me lying in different corners of the room.
(I am broken.)
He glances at the remnants of me,
His eyes welling up with tears,
He looks scared and he runs away.
I look around sorrowfully,
There's no one in the room; just the broken me.
I hear the door of the room creaking open,
(Someone came!)
It's the potter, my creator.
I see a spark of possibility,

(Maybe she will repair me!)
I wait for her to notice me,
And when she does, she walks towards me.
However, on her way she picks up the broom and the dust pan,
(No,no,no,NO,NO!)
She collects the broken me in the dust pan and mercilessly throws me into the trash can like *her* creation held no value to her.
And I lie there,
Alone in the dark and silent eternal nothingness.

48. Topper

They say your skills don't improve abruptly,
They take time,
And they do.
I know this because as a child,
I was never bright.
I was one of those children who were scolded every day,
The ones who were never liked.
I was child teachers always complained about,
I was the child my family didn't like talking about,
I was the child who stood last in the class.
But, I was the child who never knew how to give up,
I was the child who kept trying,
I was the child who tried fighting the times,
And so I was the child that won.
All of this took time,
I climbed the ladder to success step-by-step,
It was scary and hard,
I would often stumble but I never gave up,
And now I am somehow the topper!

49. Blank Page

They say that every newborn is a blank page,
That every newborn is like a piece of clay.
It's the parents or the guardians who decide how one will be moulded,
Or what shall be written in those cute little books' pages.
It's all upto them,
They are the ones who either make you an aesthetic piece of pottery,
Or a piece that was broken but looked wonderful in their eyes.
They are the ones who decide if you will be the book with happy stories,
Or the book with the tragic ones.
You decide all of this,
You shape our foundational personalities,
Then why do you still blame us for our incompetencies,
Because, honestly they just reflect yours.
So, if you are looking for anyone to blame,
If you are looking for the one who truly made mistakes,
Blame yourselves.

50. Happiness

Happiness is the caterpillar turning into a butterfly and leaving its cocoon,
Happiness is the sound of the leaves rustling on the trees when the wind blows through.
Happiness is the sound of the raindrops pattering on my rooftop,
It goes: tip-tap, tip tap-tip, tap.
Happiness is the sunrise and sunset you are lucky enough to see at the beach,
Happiness resides in the hugs you receive,
And the kisses you shower your loved ones with.
Happiness is the sunshine invading your room and waking you up in the morning after a stormy night.
Happiness is admiring the full moon at night while the world sleeps,
Happiness is when your mother lets you have an extra scoop of ice cream after dinner that one night.
However, happiness is fragile,
It is like the sand castle you build on the beach,
All it takes is one wave for it come crashing down and then you start to weep,
But you see your father, in his hand an ice cream.
And soon the indicator of happiness spreads wide across your face; you are smiling.
Happiness is a long word found in the little things.

www.ingramcontent.com/pod-product-compliance
Lightning Source LLC
LaVergne TN
LVHW041238150826
845673LV00008B/2428
* 9 7 9 8 8 9 6 1 0 0 9 0 4 *